THE WISE BARISTA

DANIEL M. LEWIS

Dedication

To the cold cup of coffee that sparked a rebellion in my taste buds and a revolution in my outlook on life. May we all learn to appreciate life's moments, hot or cold, good or bad, and never take a single sip for granted.

Table Of Contents

Preface

Do you take your coffee black or with cream? Oh, you hate coffee?

You know what, it doesn't even matter and to be honest I'm more of a tea person myself.

The truth is this book is not about coffee or tea.

This book is about you. It's about how you journey through this mysterious thing called life, how you cultivate a successful mindset towards business and relationships and how you can make your life better.

Not perfect, better.

I was inspired to write this book after receiving a lukewarm cup of coffee one morning while running errands with a friend. I took one sip of the arctic java and immediately asked my friend to turn the car around so I could have the coffee remade. After receiving a fresh hot brew, I thought "Life is hard. The week is hard. Business is challenging. The kids can drive you crazy. And so, I REFUSE to let life take this one special moment from me. I WILL ENJOY MY COFFEE!"

Later that day, my rant about how nothing was going to ruin my coffee lingered in my mind. And then it hit me. What if we viewed life the same way I viewed this coffee experience? What if we took the same stance with our well-being, relationships or even our business? How different would things be? How much more enriching would these experiences feel? And that's how this book was born.

A collection of thoughts and perspectives to help you live a more enriched life. As you read through the book, I'll occasionally switch between a fictional story used to present the concepts in a conversational way and then at times I'll add my thoughts on the same topic. This transition will sometimes occur halfway through a chapter. When this occurs, my thoughts will be identified with the heading: *'Author's Thoughts'* in italics to make it very easy for you to determine the narrative change.

I want to thank you in advance for yourtime and I do hope this book will give you value and perhaps change your perspective on a few things about life, business and everything else that makes the world go round.

So, here's to making a better coffee. Let's get started.

Acknowledgments

Thank you to my beautiful wife Renata, who never lets me read my manuscript for more than 5 seconds without interrupting me with suggested edits. Why don't you just write the book for goodness sakes. I love you 'Sqweedle' (Pet name)

To my extremely wise parents whose words are so impactful, challenging, inspiring and thought provoking that it consistently propels me to dig deeper in every aspect of my life. Dad, Mom... You embody the definition of an enriched life. You make simplicity so luxurious, and you make the act of kindness and the life of service to others the most compelling lifestyle I've ever seen.

To my two, handsome little princes' Jacob and Benjamin. You make me strive to do better and become a better person. Your little soft faces and bright personalities are everything a father could ever wish for. I am doing my best to live an exemplary life because of you. When you become grown men, I want you to say with 100% confidence that your dad is who he said he is and when you see me, you'll also see the result of amazing grandparents.

Chapter 1

The Ingredients

Heidi stepped into the quaint little café on Main. St. and was immediately enveloped by the comforting scent of freshly roasted coffee beans. The space was cozy, with warm lighting and soft music playing in the background. Heidi placed her regular order: A double long espresso with one sugar cube and then made her way to a small table near the window, where she could watch the hustle and bustle of the busy street outside while savoring her drink. As she settled in, she noticed Mark walking towards her, his warm smile shining brightly. Mark was the kind-hearted barista who worked most days at the cafe and lived just a stone's throw away. He was a friendly and personable man with a contagious positive energy, who always made everyone feel at home with his welcoming demeanor. Mark's quick wit and infectious laugh easily put Heidi at ease, making her forget about her busy day and immerse herself in the peaceful ambiance of the cafe.

"Good evening, Heidi," Mark said warmly. "It's great to see you again. How's the coffee?"

Heidi let out a sigh of relief. "It's – It's exactly what I needed."

Mark grinned. "Long day?"

"Ugh. That's an understatement. I just don't get people sometimes! Like did you read the job description before applying? Seriously…" Heidi complained.

"Ah. Work drama?" Mark replied.

Heidi chuckled. "I'm sorry, I didn't mean to throw all of my frustrations on you. I just don't understand for the life of me why some people do the things they do. You come to the office every day, you see how we work... You'd think after six months the person would catch on. The VP of sales is a piece of work. She's so different from everybody else in our department and it's so difficult working with her."

"Different? Is that such a bad thing?" Asked Mark.

"Yes! When you join a company that's been in operation for over sixty years and we've always done things a certain way, different can make you stand out like a sore thumb." Heidi replied.

"So you're not a fan of her ingredients.." Said Mark.

"Her what?" Heidi replied a bit confused.

Mark explained. "If you really think about it, we are pretty complex beings. Things are never really quite right for us. When the sun beats down on us, we complain that it's too hot. If the sun hides and the cool breeze sets in, we complain that it's too cold. Fast food is too slow and long weekends are too short. We can be very difficult to please with our ever-increasing needs, preferences and complexities. But although we may be super difficult to satisfy, we are still wonderful beings, and it will take thousands of years to fully comprehend our make-up and design."

Heidi listened intently yet baffled at where Mark was going with his point.

Mark continued. "You may think I've just painted a troubled picture of the human race that is always needy or spoiled. But my intention was to highlight some of the ways we display our differences and peculiarities and preferences when it comes to living a comfortable and enjoyable life. Sure, we're all kind of odd and unusual, we're colourful and unique, weird and special and sometimes straight up incomprehensible. But when put together in different combinations and with different proportions these are the ingredients that make up the amazing recipes of who we are."

"Hmm. That's an interesting thought. Are you sure you're not a psychiatrist on the weekends?" Heidi joked.

The pair giggled.

"So, are you suggesting I pretend everything's ok with this colleague despite the obvious disconnect between her and the rest of our team? I mean, what if the "ingredients" are just wrong? Heidi asked.

Mark slipped his fingers under his chin and gave a gentle stroke like a monk in deep thought before looking up at Heidi with enlightened eyes as if a brilliant idea had just dawned on him.

Finally, Mark asked, "Do you eat Italian?"

"Of course!" Said Heidi.

Mark responded, "If people were like gourmet meals or a special cuisine, our personalities and tendencies would be defined as the ingredients – everything that's blended to make up who we are. Everything from our culture and traditions, likes and dislikes, skills and gifts, these contribute to every aspect of our lives and the ways we choose to live, work and play. If I tried to describe my own personality by ingredients, I'd fall somewhere between fun, Caribbean cuisine, with a hint of spice. Oh! And maple syrup drizzled on top.

Why the syrup? Asked Heidi.

"Because my wife says I can be sweet at times."

Heidi giggled.

Mark continued.

"Every meal consists of a combination of ingredients in the same way every person is a combination of characteristics and traits. When we eat, we typically don't stop and try to distinguish every single ingredient that went into making a dish. But for some reason we often find ourselves holding a microscopic lens towards people trying to figure out everything they do and say and how they reason and why. We do this in an obsessive attempt to break down all the elements of their personalities and behaviors rather than accepting them as a whole. We do it to people and we do it to ourselves. Why am I like this? Why does she do that? Why, why, why? It would certainly take the joy out of eating, if we had to make a thesis on the purpose for every ingredient that was added to a specific food. Instead, we simply accept it or not, eat it or leave it alone."

Heidi was deeply considering the things Mark was saying. She kept silent and nudged him to continue talking with her eyes and so he did.

"Here's a question for you. When you find a food that you absolutely love, but when you turn the package around and look at the nutrition label, you see ingredients that you can't even pronounce... 'Xylogliceride,' 'Phxyogellium,' You know the ones. Do you toss it? Or do you keep on munching?

"Uhh...Guilty, I keep on munching." Heidi answered.

"Likewise, we often come across people with personalities and traits that we don't fully understand, what do you do then? Do you toss them? Or do you keep on getting to know them by trying to enjoy their company?

"Hmph." Heidi began stroking her chin as well faintly nodding her head.

Mark gave her a second and then concluded his thought.

"The main point I'm trying to make is that we're so accepting of the things we don't know or understand when it comes to what we allow in our bodies, yet we find it so difficult to accept people we don't know or understand into our hearts or into our world. And why? Because we suddenly become more interested in all the individual ingredients, rather than the "recipe" as a whole. This perspective has personally helped me make better conclusions about people I don't quite understand. Also, it helps me to stay clear of comparing myself to others."

Heidi took a sip of her espresso and looked out the window.

"Uh, I don't know what to say Mark. You are..." She paused. "Some barista."

"Thank you." Mark replied.

"Perhaps I need to be a bit more open minded about the "ingredients" of those around me, rather than just comparing everyone to what I call normal." Heidi concluded and continued enjoying her coffee.

Author's Thoughts: Comparisons

When it comes to comparing my life, achievements, possessions, successes and even my failures to anyone else, I remind myself that my journey is unique to me, so there's no sense in comparing. If you think about it, for me to accurately compare myself to you, we would have to be born at the same time, in the same place, raised by the same people and experienced the same things, at the same time to even begin to make any true comparisons. Any deviation in our journey automatically makes the comparison like apples to oranges. By adding or reducing even an inch of salt or sugar to any recipe, the final result will taste different. You and I are completely unique by design. Knowing this makes it useless to compare myself to you or to anyone for that matter. If I want ALL the good experiences that you've had, then I must also accept ALL the bad experiences that you've endured, since both have been crucial in shaping who you are and how you live.

Appreciation

Have you ever heard of the term terroir? Terroir refers to the characteristics, taste and flavours that are infused by the natural environment in which a food item is produced. Like wine, coffee connoisseurs enjoy the enchanting experience of swooshing the beverage around on their palate as they do their best to describe what they taste and where they believe the plant or herb was grown. It's very poetic to hear a tea sommelier describe their tasting experience of a rare, luxurious tea. Take for instance my personal tasting notes from an organic black tea I was able to source from the misty mountains of Thailand:

"Earthy-woodsy base notes, with a brilliant hint of sweet, rich honey and a whispering tail note of plums and figs. Smooth on the palate, little to no astringency, medium bodied and enjoyable for 2-3 infusions."

Are you snapping your fingers yet?

Alongside the mastery of the growers who have perfected their craft in cultivating these plants and herbs, the terroir is mainly responsible for flavour profiles that the consumer is privileged to enjoy. This means when you enjoy a terroir coffee, tea, wine or cheese, you are appreciating the climate, the soil, the country, the region and all aspects of the natural environment that have impacted the taste of that drink.

What if we had the same appreciation for ourselves or for other people? After all, we are products of the experiences we have experienced. Everything that has happened in your life up until this very moment can be referred to as your "terroir" and is responsible for your unique flavour.

Self-appreciation instils self-worth not self-focus.

Understanding that you are unique and special makes you feel good about yourself while also expanding your appreciation of others.

As Heidi left the cozy little cafe, she couldn't help but reflect on all the wisdom Mark had shared with her. She was struck by the idea that, just like in cooking, people and personalities are made up of many different ingredients, and it's up to each of us to see the beauty and uniqueness in it.

She thought about the comparisons and appreciations that Mark had talked about, and how our experiences could make all the difference in how we live our lives. She realized that she wanted to be more intentional about embracing her own ingredients in a way that would bring joy and fulfillment to her life, instead of trying to single out the differences of those around her.

Just then, she spotted a quote painted on the wall of the cafe, and it all clicked into place: "Life is a recipe, make it a good one." Heidi smiled, feeling inspired and grateful for the chance encounter with Mark. She made a mental note to come back to the cafe and have another chat with the wise barista, knowing that she would always have something new to learn from him. Finally, Heidi glanced up at the quote one last time, smiled and then she headed home.

Chapter 2

Measurement

How much coffee do you need to make the perfect cup? Well, it really depends on who you ask. A coffee lover might tell you that 1 tablespoon is needed for a lighter coffee while two tablespoons will give you that bolder taste. On the other hand, a trained barista might suggest 2.5 tablespoons is the best way to bring that java to life. To be honest, there's no right or wrong answer, but it does create a good segway into the topic of measurement.

"Measurement is the first step that leads to control and eventually to improvement." – H. James Harrington."

When it comes to tracking progress the old saying goes, "You can't improve, what you can't measure." The first three words sound like something a pessimistic coach would say to a hopeless athlete, "You can't improve..." Yet, if the struggling athlete gives an open ear to rest of the quote, they might understand what the coach is actually saying... "You can't improve, what you can't measure." The coach isn't saying you can't improve period, so give up. The coach is saying it's impossible to get better at something if you don't know how good or how bad at it you are.

Improvement is usually associated with something bad getting better. If a runner were slow, improvement would suggest they got faster. If a meal tasted awful, improvement would suggest it now tastes delicious. But can someone be fast and still get faster? Can a meal taste delicious and still get tastier? Improvement doesn't only measure one extreme to the next. Improvement is gradual progress and incremental growth. This can happen at any stage of a developing process

But in order to see where you are and where you are headed you need to establish a benchmark. A point of reference that you can look to, in order to see that you have grown or gotten better. This is where measurement steps in and says, "Remember the last time you ran that 100m sprint? Well, your time was 10.39 seconds, this time you clocked in at 10 seconds. That's a .39 second improvement." If you're familiar with 100m sprints, then you'll agree that 10 seconds is a pretty impressive time. Yet, it can still be improved on since we know the fastest 100m sprint is 9.58 set by Olympic Gold Medalist Usain Bolt. In this case, we were able to see the incremental growth or progress in time because we measured the previous run. Being fast is not the end all for a fast runner; measurement is necessary for the fast runner to get faster. Not knowing the measurement prevents the sprinter from coming to their full potential.

Is your full potential realized? The answer will depend on how good of a job you've done at measuring and keeping track of your progress.

In 2019 I read two books. In 2020 that number jumped to four. At the time of writing this book (mid-way through 2021) I have already completed over ten books. I made the decision to start reading more books in hopes of gaining new perspectives about life and all my other interests. After making the decision to read more, I noticed some amazing changes. I started to become more knowledgeable on topics that had a direct effect on my life, especially in the area of my finances and productivity. As I read more books, I began to earn more income in my business ventures, and I also became more productive with my time. I said to myself, "If reading one book can improve my finances by X amount of dollars or my productivity by X amount of time, then what if I read two books? Or three? Or six?" In some weird yet proven way, I was able to measure my personal development by the number of books I read. I'm in no way suggesting there is a mathematical calculation that you can use to guarantee more money... I'm simply saying that every time I finished a book and began implementing strategies and making changes that I learned through its content, I got better. Now, I like to use books read as a unit of measurement.

Units Of Measurement

"I'm a leader, I'm a liter like a thousand milliliters."

A unit of measurement is a definite magnitude of quantity which helps us measure things. Scientifically speaking, these units are pretty set it stone as we've used them for thousands of years to measure things. For example: kg, m, ml etc.

Now I'm certainly not challenging science when I say this, but why can't we establish other units of measurement to track progress in our lives? Units like: positive impact, self-fulfillment, community contribution or just general happiness?

Of course, this is nothing new to the SDSN better known as the Sustainable Development Solutions Network – A global initiative for the United Nations. This organization was responsible for the World Happiness Report, which was created back in 2011 with the goal of measuring the overall happiness and satisfaction of the people living within a given country. The SDSN's hope for this initiative was to learn what determining factors were contributing to people's happiness and satisfaction in their lives. If they could measure people's happiness, then they could also improve it and use the information to help guide public policy. Finland has enjoyed its spot at the top for the last 4 years, being dubbed "The World's Happiest Country, even after going through the harsh setbacks caused by COVID-19.

It's enlightening to know that measurement isn't restricted to science and that it can be used to track the overall progress of anything we seek to improve. That includes your health, your finances, and your contribution to society, your relationships and even your happiness.

Maybe you're at the stage in your life where you feel that you've got all the ingredients necessary to make something special, to change the world or even surprise yourself. But remember the right ingredients don't make the best cakes, the right measurements do. If it can be measured, it can be improved.

Chapter 3

The Espresso Mindset

Heidi walked into the coffee shop; her mind preoccupied with her day ahead. As she approached the counter, she suddenly heard a familiar voice. It was Mark, the barista who had made her a double espresso on her last visit.

"Hey, Heidi! Good to see you again," Mark greeted her with a smile.

"Good to see you too, Mark. How's life treating you?" Heidi asked.

"It's going well, thanks for asking. How about you? How's work been?" Mark asked.

"It's been busy, but good. I'm actually here for another double espresso today. You made a great one for me last time," Heidi complimented.

"Thanks, I'm glad you liked it. You know, making the perfect cup of coffee-like life is all about consistency. It takes the right amount of ingredients, pressure, and technique, executed consistently, to get the desired result," Mark said, as he started preparing Heidi's drink.

"Yes, I've heard that before. But what do you mean by consistency in life?" Heidi asked, intrigued.

"Well, it's the same principle as making the perfect espresso. To be successful in life, you need to consistently put in the effort, practice, and have a disciplined mindset. You can't expect to achieve your goals with just one big effort," Mark explained.

Heidi nodded in agreement. "It reminds me of a famous Bruce Lee quote, 'I fear not the man who has practiced 10,000 kicks once, but I fear the man who has practiced one kick 10,000 times.' It's so true."

"Exactly," Mark said. "Consistency is key. And when you're consistent, not only will you get better at something, but you'll also cultivate an attitude of discipline, which will help in many other areas of life. Effort is not enough, it's consistent effort that counts. And when things don't work out, it's important to not get discouraged. It's just a bump in the road, a lump in your matcha, if you will."

Heidi chuckled.

Mark continued. "The great thing about cultivating the habit of discipline is that it comes with an autopilot function. When things are not working out for you or when faced with a difficult challenge, a disciplined mindset will kick in and you'll find yourself doing what's necessary to improve the situation and get better results." Mark added.

"That's so true," Heidi said, as she took a sip of her double espresso. "Thanks, Mark, for the wise words once again.

I think I'll keep the espresso mindset in mind in my pursuit of a better life."

Mark smiled. "I'm glad I could help. And remember, consistency is key."

Heidi nodded and gave a big smile and went to find a seat.

Author's Thoughts: Espresso Mindset

When it comes to living a successful life, it is important to have an espresso mindset. It will take a consistent concentrated effort to create something you love. I absolutely cherish the occasional shot of espresso. I don't know if it's the thickness of the liquor when it's poured or the boost of caffeine I get from a single shot. Honestly, it could even be that the espresso cups are just so tiny and cute. Whatever it is, I have become so fascinated by the art of the espresso that I was determined to find out what it takes to pull the perfect shot and then see if there were any key takeaways that could be applied to living a better life.

Article after article, barista after barista, the same tips were being offered and it became obvious that regardless of the technique, type of coffee grounds or equipment you use, the key to making the perfect shot of espresso was found in the word 'consistency.' The most celebrated coffee shops are not appreciated because the barista can make an impressive espresso; they're appreciated because they can make an impressive espresso all the time.

To be successful in anything, a person must harness the ability to repeat an activity to the point of mastery. Mastery refers to unlocking a level of achievement that was once believed to be unachievable, to self. To a person embarking on a personal development journey, mastery is more about capability then superiority over someone else. Remember you're working on you and I'm working on me.

Consistency is a hyper understanding that no single effort can bring about success; it will require repetition to attain your best. The amazing thing about consistency, is not only will a person get better at something the more they practice it, but they will also cultivate an attitude of discipline which will assist in many other important aspects of living a wholesome life. Effort won't cut it. Consistent effort will. Practice won't do it. Consistent practice will. A person who digs is unlikely to find treasure, but a person who consistently digs likely will.

To be successful it will take the right amount of ingredients, the right amount of pressure technique and skill executed consistently. This is the espresso mindset.

Chapter 4

Filtered Coffee

Have you ever thought about the purpose of using a filter when brewing coffee? It's to separate its rich liquor from the unwanted coffee grounds to make sure that what you're drinking is pure and delicious. It's interesting to think that the same coffee grounds that you were once so excited to purchase and brew, are now being filtered out to make sure they don't end up in your cup.

But this concept extends far beyond coffee. In life, we are constantly bombarded with information, experiences, and people's perspectives. Some of it is good, some of it is bad, and some of it is just unnecessary. The lesson to be learned here is that just because something may look good, taste good, feel good, or be expensive, it doesn't mean that we need to have it or at least all of it. Sometimes, it's better to extract what we need and discard the rest.

For instance, it's great to catch up with an old friend and chat about life, but conversations about how annoying or frustrating a co-worker can be, or how devastating it is to sit through a meeting with your boss, may not be something you need to share or be exposed to. Even this very book may present concepts, some of which may resonate with you, while others may not. It's important to filter out what you don't need and focus on what's truly essential. Author George McKeown once quoted, "Where is the wisdom we have lost in knowledge? Where is the knowledge we have lost in information?" It's important to be responsible for what we let in and what we filter out.

A filtered life is understanding that not everything we see is meant for our eyes, and not everything we hear is beneficial to our ears. To lead a wholesome life, we must make firm decisions on what we let into our minds, our space, and our hearts, as failure to filter will make for a terrible cup of coffee. Without a filter, there will be excess. A filter separates the desired from the undesired, the necessary from the unnecessary, and at times, the good from the bad. By filtering out what really matters from what doesn't, we can avoid burdening ourselves with annoying little fragments of things that can make life distasteful and unpleasant.

While writing this book, I remember sitting in a local coffee shop where I pulled out my laptop ready to tackle several tasks. I ordered my usual dark roast, black-no cream, no sugar and decided to turn it into a small brunch by pairing it with a tuna salad sandwich. Excited to get to work, I grabbed my phone and set my pomodoro timer, hit start and began typing away. Shortly after, a pleasant lady pulled up a chair at the table beside me. She pulled out her phone and began scrolling away on some app that was obviously keeping her entertained, I could tell by the faint chuckles she unsuccessfully tried to conceal every few seconds. About five minutes after the lady took a seat, another woman entered the café with such a level of excitement, that she caused everyone to stop what they were doing and watch the two ladies tightly embrace each other, rocking side to side and belting out how much they missed each other. It was quite beautiful to see.

It had only been two weeks since the province of Ontario loosened restrictions on the COVID-19 lockdowns, so these two ladies hadn't seen each other in a long time. The simple pleasure of sitting in a café and pulling out your laptop had now felt like a rare luxury. As the two women grabbed their drinks and sat down, they immediately began engaging in a conversation that was impossible to ignore as they spoke at volumes you'd hear at a nightclub. I tried my best to stay focused as my twenty-five-minute timer was ticking away.

Then it happened!

About two and half minutes into their conversation, they suddenly began trash talking every single co-worker, neighbor, manager, politician and relative including their children! I had just witnessed a bloodbath of words. What had happened to the pleasant looking women that met up to share a cup of coffee and catch up after a challenging year of lockdowns? Where did the smiles and laughter go? What were these ladies expecting to gain from this conversation that could add value to their lives? I was blown away and after trying to block them out, I grabbed my headphones and cued my lo-fi instrumentals. I sighed with relief, as their voices became faint noise in the background.

What a toxic conversation I thought to myself. Here were two women, decked in beautiful summer dresses, sitting for brunch in a chic café and all they do was gossip about other people, who have no clue that they're being spoken of in this way. Thank goodness I was able to filter their conversation out with my music.

This situation sheds light on a very important aspect of life that relates to the filtered coffee perspective, the power of words. They're powerful enough to break the toughest of egos and inspiring enough to rebuild the most broken hearts. If not carefully considered, words can cause serious damage. Damage to those who speak harmful words and especially to those who hear them.

When people speak doubtful and harassing words around you, filter them out. When friends or colleagues approach you and try to lure you into a gossiping session against your boss, change the conversation or walk away. When the words of a book, show, magazine or the ones that formulate in your own mind try to present toxic or destructive narratives, find a way to filter. If you have to listen to relaxing music to change the tone, do it. If you have to switch the TV off, do it. Close the app, switch your seat and make new friends if it means that. Because the long-term effect that negativity words can have on a person, may contaminate your heart and cause bitterness, hopelessness and discouragement in ways that are incredibly difficult to repair. Filter your coffee, to enjoy your coffee.

Chapter 5

Coffee Stains

[How to live an impactful life]

"Our fingerprints never fade from the lives we've touched."
– Judy Blume.

By definition the word **impact** means the act of one object coming forcibly into contact with another. This is exactly what happens when we connect with people and leave a meaningful mark in their life. Our ability to affect others can be a beautiful blessing or a terrible curse depending on the kind of impression we choose to leave. I like to view impact as an intangible gift that I leave behind with every interaction that I have, every day. The very fact that this "gift" is invisible makes it completely up to the other person to discover and enjoy it. After all, you won't impact every single person you encounter but that shouldn't change your intention of leaving a positive mark.

Living an impactful life is a conscious decision that we make once we understand the consequences that our life can have on another. Nothing tells the story of impact better than an article I stumbled on written by Robert Tew on his site LiveLifeHappy.com. Robert shared an unforgettable story about an eighty-seven-year-old college student named Rose, who on her first day in class looked around to introduce herself to other students. "Get to know someone and learn something you never knew." said the professor, and Rose wasted no time at all. A young student recalls feeling a soft gentle tap on his shoulder only to turn around and find a wrinkled, old woman with a smile that illuminated the room.

"Hi handsome," she said. "My name is Rose, I'm eighty-seven years old. Can I give you a hug?"

The surprised young man laughed and responded, "Of course!" as he was sucked into her tight embrace.

"Why are you in college at such a young, innocent age?" he playfully asked.

"I'm here to meet a rich husband, get married and have a couple of kids..." They both laughed.

By now he understood that Rose had a good sense of humor, but he remained curious as to her motivation at such a mature age. Rose settled the young man's curiosity by letting him know that she had always dreamed of getting her college education and that the opportunity had finally presented itself.

After class they decided to go for lunch and enjoy a chocolate milkshake. They became instant friends and over the next three months, would leave class together and strike up conversations about everything. The young man referred to their conversations like listening to a time machine of wisdom and experience.

Over the next year, Rose became the campus icon making friends with everyone she encountered while enjoying the special attention garnered by the peculiarity of her age and enrollment in college. In fact, she became so popular that the young man invited her to speak at his football team's banquet. He recalls her giving a speech that he will never forget. Rose was introduced and she stepped to the podium. As she stepped to the microphone, she accidently dropped her cue cards on the floor. Frustrated and a little embarrassed she leaned into the microphone and said,

"I'm sorry I'm so jittery. I gave up beer for Lent and this whiskey is killing me! I'll never get my speech back in order so let me just tell you what I know."

The crowd eased her nerves with a gentle laugh as she cleared her throat and began her speech.

"We do not stop playing because we are old; we grow old because we stop playing. There are only four secrets to staying young, being happy, and achieving success. You have to laugh and find humor every day. You've got to have a dream. When you lose your dreams, you die. We have so many people walking around who are dead and don't even know it. There is a huge difference between growing older and growing up. If you are nineteen years old and lie in bed for one full year and don't do one productive thing, you will turn twenty years old. If I am eighty-seven years old and stay in bed for a year and never do anything I will turn eighty-eight. Anybody can grow older. That doesn't take any talent or ability. The idea is to grow up by always finding opportunity in change. Have no regrets. The elderly usually don't have regrets for what we did, but rather for things we did not do. The only people who fear death are those with regrets."

She concluded her speech by courageously singing the song called, 'The Rose' – By Bette Midler and then challenged the students to study the lyrics and live by the words of the song.

At the end of the year, Rose had finally completed the college degree that she had always dreamed of achieving.

One week after graduation, Rose died peacefully in her sleep. Over two thousand college students attended her funeral to pay their tribute to the woman who taught by example that it's never too late to be all you can possibly be and achieve everything you've always dreamed of.

Robert concludes the article with a thought-provoking quote, "Remember, growing old is mandatory, growing up is optional. We make a living by what we get, we make a life by what we give."

Rose undoubtedly left her mark in the world by impacting the lives of so many, and Robert has also impacted others by sharing this inspirational story and many others through his blog site. (donations can be made to support his efforts.) I intend to continue the chain of positive impact with the content found in this book. What will your contribution be? How will you begin or continue to bring about positive change in the lives of others? You don't need any external or tangible materials to do it; you just need to decide. Decide to live an impactful life every day, with everyone, everywhere you go. In a way, living an impactful life is like a coffee stain. It never really fades away.

Chapter 6

Out Of Cream

"A bend in the road is not the end of the road... unless you fail to make the turn." – Helen Keller.

Have you ever gotten out of bed with a desperate desire to get to your morning coffee? You speed through your morning routine, brushing your teeth, combing your hair, while getting dressed simultaneously, just to get in your sacred chair and tightly grip that hot cup of java. The rich smell of coffee beans fills the air as your kitchen slowly transforms into a local coffee shop. At last, the coffee's ready. You pull out your favourite mug, the one that manages to make your coffee look and taste better, a theory you sold yourself but know in the back of your mind isn't true. Your heart smiles while you fill your mug and observe the f lavourful bubbles grouping together ready to explode on your palate. You walk over to the fridge, open the door and BOOM! It hits you. You're out of cream.

There aren't many things in life as disappointing as this. I only know this from observation not from experience as I drink my coffee black. My wife Renata on the other hand is a cream connoisseur and always insists on adding at least one tablespoon to her brew, but what happens when you're out of cream? Can you still enjoy your coffee? Better yet, what happens when things don't go as planned; can you still enjoy your life?

When I was 18, I dropped out of high school to put a tighter grip on my dream of becoming a world-famous hip-hop artist. I was confident in my ability to write songs and I loved performing on stage. I to build a respectable name for myself in the local rap scene. And I was daring and willing to do whatever it took to standout to get recognized by a top recording label, always reassuring myself that I was a star in the making and there was no way I wouldn't "Make it."

High School?

Why on earth would I sit down in a preppy school uniform listening to a teacher explain fractions and algebra, when I could be in the studio writing my next hit? My parents would come to realize that they had given birth to a "golden child" who was going to take them straight to Beverly Hills to live "that good life." I couldn't waste any more time in school, I had to get things moving. Grammy-award-winning-hip-hop artist- Daniel Lewis...This was destiny I could feel it.

A few months after leaving high school, I started my first day at a Winners factory warehouse stacking boxes and filling trailers.

"A loser working at Winners, ha-hardy-ha-ha..."

I lasted two weeks at Winners before moving on to work at another warehouse, then a manufacturing company that made paper tubes, then a company who paints things. I was a lot jockey, a dishwasher, a line cook at various restaurants including a Chinese Restaurant (who made the best fried rice by the way.) and I eventually ended up working in a garbage bin sorting nails and screws. Not the kind of hit song I had in mind. Clearly, my plan had failed. I was not an award-winning hip-hop artist. My parents were not living in Beverley Hills. I didn't graduate from high school. I had no career, no back-up plan, and certainly no money.

I was out of cream.

It's very natural for the next pages of my life to have turned very dark and bitter. But every time things didn't go as planned (which was far too often,) I was somehow still able to create a new plan. I didn't know it then, but even in the complete chaos of the life I was living, jumping from job to job and trying a little of this and a little of that, I was building a skill that would prove to be valuable above any degree: Resilience.

I know we don't normally refer to people who seem confused as resilient, but this unsurety taught me the invaluable lesson of how to bounce back. It's the very definition of what being resilient means. When you're out of cream you learn to enjoy your coffee black. When life doesn't go as planned, you change the plan. Resilient, determined, optimistic; it really doesn't matter what you call it, but this attitude can be extremely beneficial when you consider the uncertainty we face every single day.

American writer Claire Cook once said, "If plan 'A' fails, don't worry you still have 24 more letters in the alphabet. 204 if you're in Japan." This is exactly the kind of attitude we should cultivate when it comes to the bends in the road. Of course, we should make plans, and have dreams and aspirations and get excited to make the perfect coffee. But we should always be mindful that things don't always work out the way we think they should.

Today, I've successfully published four books. I've launched three businesses, which have generated millions of dollars in sales. I have beeninvited to serve tea to His Majesty King Charles III and manycelebrities and notable dignitaries. I have become a global entrepreneurship ambassador for Canada.

I sit on two executive boards and as an international speaker I have shared my story with thousands. I volunteered my time to speak in prisons and correctional facilities to inspire hope to the inmates. I've even been invited to speak at my old high school on several occasions. I am a lucky husband and a proud father of two little boys. I am a certified Tea Master Sommelier and Certified CITP (Canadian International Trade Professional.)

And while I was writing this chapter, I finally completed my High School Diploma. I never became the famous hip hop star. Nor did I take the traditional path to "success." But I still managed to accomplish some things I'm very proud of. I learned that life is not linear. Even the heart monitor shows us that. Two of the greatest skills we can develop in our livesto continue thriving instead of diving when life gets tough, is resilience and adaptability.

"My entire life can be described in one sentence: It didn't go as planned, and that's ok." – Rachel Wolchin.

Chapter 7

Cup Of Tea

[Do something different]

"If you want something different, do something different. Same crap different day doesn't describe the day, it describes your attitude about it."

– Steve Maraboli.

As a Certified Tea Master Sommelier and owner of a tea company, you'd imagine that I have drank my fair share of tea. Drinking three to four cups of Earl Grey per day isn't out of the ordinary for me. However, even with my obsession for tea, I would occasionally do away with it completely to make room for a roasted, bold coffee. (Yes, tea masters drink coffee too.) I'd assume it's the same for the coffee aficionado, who once in a while decides to set aside their favourite beans for an earthy green tea. Whatever the case, it's never good to stick to one thing, (unless of course we're talking about my wife, which… I'll stop there.)

The definition of insanity as stated by Albert Einstein, is to do the same thing and expect different results. Enjoying your coffee means that sometimes you'll have to make a cup of tea. You have to switch things up, mess up your routine, tread a new path and try something new. When thinking about embracing change and trying new things, we can learn a lot from the inspiring story of a man named Howard, who embodies the change mindset and has become a visionary because of it.

In 1971 Starbucks was founded by Jerry Baldwin, Gordon Bowker, and Zev Siegel, who opened their first store right across the street from the historic Pike's Place Market in Seattle: a fish market which is famous for throwing the daily catch at you! After discovering a genuine love and obsession for premium quality coffee beans and teas from a successful importer: Peete's Coffee & Tea based in Berkley California, the three founders decided to make Peete's their exclusive supplier.

The partnership was the perfect fit which led them to invest in new coffee roasting equipment from Holland that allowed them to explore and perfect their unique roasting method. They expanded into four stores by the early 1980's which confirmed that the men had struck BOLD... or gold, rather. At this time, Zev Siegel decided to leave the company to pursue other interests. One year after the expansion in 1981, a savvy sales representative from a Swedish kitchenware distributor decided to pay its thriving client a visit. His name was Howard Shultz. During his visit, Howard was captivated by the coffee chain's success and loyal customer base. Howard also noticed a few areas of the operation that could use some improvement, so he offered to work for the company to be able to inf luence the changes that he believed would make Starbucks an even greater success. Shortly after, Howard was hired as Starbuck's Marketing and Advertising Director.

In the spring of 1983, after returning from an inspirational visit from Milan, Howard Shultz proposed a new direction to the founders of Starbucks', which was driven by his enchanting experiences in the daytime cafes' in Italy. Howard suggested that Starbucks shift it's focus to serving customers ready-to-drink coffees, cappuccinos and espressos rather than bulk coffee beans, teas and equipment. He felt that adapting this concept would attract even more coffee lovers to their stores. But The founders strongly disagreed with Howard's suggestion. So, Howard quit Starbucks and started his own coffee house called Il Giornale. And guess what? It became an instant success with quick expansion across several cities.

Two years later, perhaps due to the pressure of the new competition from Howard, Jerry Baldwin and Gordon Bowker decided to list Starbucks for sale. And who do you think the new buyer was? You guessed it, none other than Howard Shultz, who quickly scooped up the company and merged all of his existing cafes under the Starbucks brand.

Over the next few years, the company experienced a colossal expansion, giving them the title as the largest coffee chain in the world. Fast forward to today, Starbucks is a behemoth with north of 20,000 stores across the globe and can be found in almost every corner across North America and beyond.

As I sit here writing this on a Starbucks patio sipping my Pike's roast, I think to myself, "What would have become of Starbucks had they simply stuck to selling coffee beans and equipment?" If Howard Shultz hadn't dared to try something new, and just continued doing what they'd always done, would this great company still be around today?

Are there things in your life that are due for a change? Perhaps this is your wake-up call to consider a new beginning or to open your heart to a new path. Sometimes even the smallest of changes can have a massive impact on the course of our lives.

Like Howard Shultz, we must assess and challenge the norms that we have been accustomed to for so long and learn to become visionaries of our own lives. Only then can we begin to design a future filled with better opportunities and make room for new experiences and possibilities. Sometimes, we have to set aside the coffee and try a cup of tea.

Chapter 8

Light Roast

"Excuses will always be there for you, opportunity will not."
-Marques Ogden.

Mark, the barista, was tidying up the cafe as Heidi walked in. She looked stressed and tired.

"Hi Heidi, how are you doing today?" Mark asked, noticing the look on her face.

Heidi let out a long sigh, "I'm okay, just feeling a bit down."

"Oh no, what's been going on?" Mark asked with genuine concern.

"I just got rejected from this job I really wanted," Heidi replied, looking dejected.

"I'm sorry to hear that," Mark said sympathetically. "But don't be too hard on yourself. Rejection is tough, but it's not the end of the world. Sometimes we need to embrace the sting of disappointment and use it as motivation to do better next time."

"I know, but it's just so frustrating," Heidi said. "I feel like I've been trying so hard, but it's not enough."

Mark smiled knowingly, "I get it. But have you ever heard of the concept of a light roast?"

Heidi looked at him quizzically, "What do you mean?"

"Well, a light roast is a term I came up with to describe the idea that sometimes we need to be our own biggest critic in order to reach our full potential," Mark explained. "It's like roasting coffee beans. If you don't roast them enough, they don't reach their full f lavor potential. But if you roast them too much, they lose their unique characteristics. So, we need to find that balance where we're pushing ourselves to be better, but not to the point where we're destroying ourselves in the process."

Heidi nodded slowly, "I see what you mean. It's like I need to find that sweet spot between not pushing myself hard enough and pushing myself too hard?"

"Exactly!" Mark exclaimed. "It's all about finding that balance. And sometimes, we need to pull ourselves to that limit, rather than pushing ourselves. Pulling is like extending a hand to yourself and using your strength to lift yourself up. It's a positive and encouraging way to motivate yourself to do better."

Heidi smiled, feeling a bit better already. "Thanks, Mark. I really needed to hear that."

"Anytime, Heidi," Mark said with a smile.

"Now, how about I make you a nice cup of coffee to help you feel even better?"

Author's Thoughts: Light Roast

Has anyone ever told you "Don't be too hard on yourself?" Well, they're right. It's unhealthy to beat yourself down when you've gone through some form of defeat or didn't quite live up to an expectation. However, this comforting statement isn't meant to be taken as a free card to make excuses for poor performance or lack of effort. Sometimes we are actually too easy on ourselves, and this creates a sort of defensive shield made to protect our ego and pride. What we need to do is land somewhere in the middle. We have to learn to embrace the sting that comes with disappointment and transform it into momentum and motivation to do better the next time.

I'm not suggesting that in order to be better you must push yourself to the limit. But what if we pulled ourselves to the limit? Pulling someone is completely different than pushing someone. Pushing can be associated with bullying or manipulation. It's the bully pushing the nerd around in the school yard. Or as the well-known warning of a person about to lose their cool goes, "don't push my buttons!" There are many examples of the word pushing that tend to evoke a sense of confrontation and conflict and this is why a person shouldn't push themselves to do better.

But pulling brings thoughts of helping a person come up higher. The first thought that comes to my mind when I hear the word pulling, is a person extending their hand towards someone else and that person reaching up to grab them. Once a connection is made, the person on top uses their anchoring strength to pull the other person up and out.

Whenever I found myself in a situation where I was unsuccessful, it was that little voice inside telling me that I could do better that encouraged me to dig deeper and to pull out the extra 'umph' needed to keep going. That's the pull that you need to focus on to when it comes to excelling or getting things done. You might have had an unsuccessful run at a business you launched, rather than giving up or beating yourself down, pull yourself together, learn from your mistakes and try again with more knowledge. You're unsuccessful in getting that promotion at work that you felt you deserved? That's ok. Gain some new skills that you can pull on next time to better convince your manager that you're the right person for the role. In order to have a good pull on anything, you've got to have a good grip on it first. This chapter is basically a "Get A Grip!" kind of chapter or what I like to call a "light roast."

We could all use a light roast every now and then and I'm not referring to coffee. We need to be our biggest critic in order to properly evaluate where we're at in life and the quality of output we're putting out into the world.

Is that really the best logo concept you can come up with?

Have you really done your absolute best to give your business a chance to succeed in the marketplace?

Is that as good as it gets when it comes to an organized room, home, office or shop?

Was that the best customer service you could give?

Was that the politest way to speak to that person or handle that situation?

Is this the most productive thing you could be doing with your time right now?

It's these straightforward questions that when honestly answered would allow us to get better and grow. Give yourself a "light roast." Put yourself on trial and start to go through the fine details of your life. Your motives, your thoughts, your work ethic, consider it all and don't be afraid to drill yourself to iron out some hard truths about you. This is self-discovery and it makes room for self-improvement.

I love to call myself into question and put myself in the hot seat to correct those little things that silently yet viciously hold back my full potential. I like to lightly roast myself from time to time, not because I intend to beat myself up but because it's a great way to bring new and interesting f lavours, skills, potential and abilities that unroasted I may not have discovered.

Chapter 9

Coffee Buddy

"Hey, Heidi," Mark greeted her with a warm smile. "How are you doing today?"

"I'm okay," Heidi replied, not sounding very convincing.

Mark could tell that something was bothering her. "Is everything alright?" he asked with genuine concern.

Heidi hesitated for a moment before opening up to Mark. She told him about a disagreement she had with her colleague at work and how they couldn't seem to find a way to resolve the issue. Heidi had been blaming her colleague for not seeing things her way, and the tension between them was taking a toll on their jobs. Mark listened patiently, nodding in understanding as Heidi spoke.

"You know, Heidi," he said after she finished, "it's easy to blame others when things go wrong. But in my experience, that only leads to more problems. It's important to take responsibility for our own actions and work towards finding solutions, rather than pointing fingers."

Heidi nodded in agreement. "I know, but it's hard to do that sometimes," she said, feeling a little embarrassed about her behavior.

"I understand," Mark replied. "It takes practice, but it's worth it. When we take responsibility for our actions, we create a space for solutions to emerge. Blaming others only creates more conflict and makes it harder to find common ground."

As Heidi finished her coffee and left the coffee shop, she felt lighter and more hopeful. Mark's words had given her a new perspective on the situation, and she felt motivated to take responsibility for her part in the disagreement and work towards finding a solution with her colleague. As she walked away, Heidi thought about how her coffee buddy, Mark, had helped her see the situation in a new light. She realized that having someone to confide in and bounce ideas off was invaluable, especially when dealing with difficult situations. And so, as she continued on her way, Heidi couldn't help but think about how important it is to have healthy relationships and coffee buddies in our lives, people who can offer us a fresh perspective and support us in finding solutions to the challenges we face.

Author's Thoughts

Mom? Dad? Sibling? Colleague? Spouse? Who do you love to grab a coffee with?

There's always that person who no matter the circumstance will take time out of their day to join you for a coffee. I call that person "a coffee buddy." They are the masters of conversation, listening monks, wise elephants that speak in parables. Your coffee buddy is the person that you love to be around to enjoy a brief moment of companion-filled bliss. Coffee buddies play an integral role in living a balanced life. And so, we find ourselves at the part of the book that talks about healthy relationships.

"Let's not forget, it's you and me vs. the problem, not you vs. me." — Steve Maraboli

When we face difficult situations, it's common to look for someone to blame, someone who we believe caused the problem. This is a coping mechanism that helps us deal with the issue at hand.

For example, imagine a student who didn't study for a test and ends up failing. Instead of taking responsibility for not studying, they might blame their friends for distracting them or their teacher for not teaching the material well enough. It's easier to place the blame on someone else rather than accept our own shortcomings. This mentality is not limited to personal situations, but also to conflicts between individuals or even nations. It's a common theme in conflict resolution that parties involved tend to blame each other for the problem rather than seeking solutions. This mindset can be likened to the story of Adam and Eve from the Christian Bible. According to the story, Eve was tempted by the serpent to eat from the forbidden tree, and in turn, convinced Adam to do the same. When God confronts them about their disobedience, Adam blames Eve, saying, "The woman you put here with me—she gave me some fruit from the tree, and I ate it."

This "Eve told me to do it" mentality of blaming others for our problems is toxic and can lead to more challenges. It's important to take responsibility for our actions and work towards f inding solutions rather than perpetuating the cycle of blame. Our relationships and overall well-being are dependent on our ability to take ownership of our choices and work towards positive outcomes.

How can a person truly progress in anything while carrying the invisible weight of an unsolved issue with another person? This is a two-step forward one step backwards approach to life and the quicker we can find closure to issues, the more qualitative of a life we can live.

My wife and I built our business together. We've been 50/50 partners and have shared responsibilities from the start. People always ask, "How in the world do you work with your spouse?" I understand why this would seem like a difficult thing to do. A simple disagreement on the colour of a new product package can continue into a late-night argument at home. Who will man the tradeshow booth? Whose work is deemed "more important?" These are all very real conversations and issues that could and would arise in our everyday work life. And to make things even more interesting there are personal disagreements and arguments that begin at home that leak into work.

So, how did we do it?

We both decided to view life as much more than a set of problems and to view business as much more than a set of transactions. Business is a tool that we can use to impact the lives of others in a special way. This supersedes our personal opinions about what we think is right or wrong. In other words, we've learned to "GET OVER OURSELVES!"

There are more important things to get done than the day-to-day frustrations for us to stand around arguing. This stance has helped us stay level-headed through the storms. Every person needs a coffee buddy. A person that they can confide in and bounce ideas off, speak to and also learn from.

Whether this person is our mentor, coach, parent, teacher, spouse or friend, find and nurture those special relationships. You after all are who you hang around.

Chapter 10

Special Brew

"The secret to succeeding in business can be found in the first two letters of business...BU!"

- Daniel Lewis.

When invited to speak to an audience at any corporate conference or business focused event, I often speak on a topic that I like to call "The Power of Personality." At first glance this may not seem like your typical strategic business content or revenue generating keynote address, but boy does it have everything to do with building true success.

I begin by asking the audience: "What's the difference between a person being called childish and childlike?"

Being childish simply means: to be silly and immature and there isn't much room for this kind of behavior in our adult lives. On the other hand, we have the word "childlike." To be childlike means: to embody the common character traits, tendencies and personalities that are found in young children. Some of these traits include trustworthiness, being forgiving, fearlessness, naivety, simplicity, unbiasedness and innocence. Surprisingly these characteristics are found amongst the most successful people in the world!

Tech titan Elon Musk has been seen dancing on stages during product launches, engaging in extremely candid twitter threads and even incorporated a sense of youthful humour in Tesla's software. The whoopy cushion sound effect installed in the app allows you to prank your fellow passengers by triggering an embarrassing sound that might warrant for the window to go down or cause for a giggle at the least. Elon didn't stop there. He also added a beat making app and a paint brush sketch tool into his sought-after line of electric vehicles. And with all this "child-like" activity in motion, Elon Musk still manages to rank within the top 20 richest people in the world.

The Power of Personality.

Just like a uniquely brewed coffee, our personalities enable us to share something special with the world and really leave an impactful mark on everyone we encounter. Your personality is what makes you different, makes you stand out and understanding this is a powerful truth in and of itself.

Our personalities have been shaped since the sandbox days and although they're constantly evolving as we change, there are some core traits that should always remain the same. Unfortunately, what tends to happen in most people's lives is that as we develop and encounter other people, we start to put our own personality into question.

"Look at Tom, he's such a confident person."

"If only I could be as smart as Lisa…"

"I'm not even half as funny as Brian."

Thoughts like these slowly rip away at our self-confidence and we start to develop a protective personality shell, that helps us adapt to the "societal norms." Then poof! We have a world or workplace or community of individuals who have compromised their individuality for the sake of "fitting in."

I did the same.

From my childhood it was crystal clear that I was the entertainer in the family. The charismatic, humorous, odd-fashioned, class clown that would never shy away from a performance. And although I was very comfortable with who I was, my personality worked against me when I began my high-school journey. Have you ever wondered how to make a high school teacher or principal hate you back in the day? Simple. Just be the student in the class that is: An entertainer, charismatic, humorous, class clown and always performing. Yeah, I was basically destined to fail within that system.

And fail I did. In my last year of high school (grade twelve) I was kicked out of school for misbehavior and told that school is just not for me, I'd be better off working a general labour job or finding a trade that didn't require any academic skill. Now let's be clear, I was no angel and in no way did I disagree with their analysis of me, it's not like I wanted to be there, neither did I apply myself or give any real effort to succeed. So, there's no hard feelings. I also don't blame the old educational system as I once did, this was simply an oil and water relationship that just didn't mix well or at all.

I decided to take my teacher's advice and get a job, and for the next few years of my life I landed many high-level management positions including manager at McDonald's and General Manager of Domino's Pizza. But things got a little tricky when I made the decision to start my own business. I had no prior business experience, and no educational backing and so I figured I would just look at what other entrepreneurs were doing and do the same. They had the formal business attire; they had super complex systems and spoke the fancy business jargon and seemed extremely smart.

Then there was me...

Doing my best to follow suit and play the role of the glamorous twentieth century "entrepreneur." It was a nightmare. For the first time in my life, I began to put my personality and who I am into question. I felt that If I didn't "play the part" and "look the part" then I wouldn't be successful. I felt that I needed to trade in the f lamboyant, colourful clothes for more business casual attire. Less stripes, polka dots and patterns and more blacks, blues and greys. I felt that it was more appropriate to refrain from asking questions in meetings even though I had no clue what they we're talking about. I wasn't being me and it was awkward, uncomfortable and I hated it. But I strongly believed this was necessary to be successful in business. How wrong I was. After more than a year of the Daniel facade, I had a life changing conversation with my dad who explained to me the difference between being childish and childlike and encouraged me not to lose those childlike qualities that he and my mom knew so well and had witnessed since my early sandbox days.

"Use it. Incorporate it into your business." My dad said.

So, I did, and my business began to grow substantially. I started attending meetings with a funky bowtie on and knee high, waldo-striped socks, I would dress up in superhero costumes at the local farmers market and even for the occasional keynote presentation (I repeat occasional.) I would be straight up with potential business prospects and during negotiations when it came to the overly complicated business jargon, I would just say, "to be honest, I don't really understand what that means." This is where I found success, true success on my terms, according to my definition and most importantly while being true to myself.

Perhaps you're a humorous person, or maybe you're more of an introverted observer, maybe you like to express yourself in numbers, words, art or poetry, maybe you're a visual learner or straight up genius. Whatever or whoever you are, learn to celebrate that, use it to change the world or at least to change your world and never compromise your personality just to "fit in." This is the power of personality and if you practice being comfortable sharing it, then it can truly be enjoyed by you and the rest of the world, sort of like a special cup of coffee.

Chapter 11

Empty Mug

"How do you add more coffee into a cup that is already filled to the brim? You pour it out first."

– Daniel Lewis

Mark, the wise barista, was in the midst of his morning routine, carefully preparing his signature espresso shots for his regular customers. He had been doing this for years and it had become second nature to him. He was focused, but he always had an ear open for those who needed it. Heidi walked into the coffee shop with a smile on her face. She had been coming there for quite some time now and had built a strong friendship with Mark. She walked up to the counter and ordered her usual latte. Mark smiled at her and began preparing her drink. As he handed her the latte, he noticed a sadness in her eyes. He asked her, "Is everything okay, Heidi?" She paused for a moment, then opened up to Mark. She told him about her continuous struggles with her career and how she felt like she was at a dead-end. Mark listened intently, then spoke up.

"You know, Heidi, when you're feeling lost or stuck, the best thing you can do is give yourself to others. Pour yourself out and give what you can. It may seem counterintuitive, but it's often the best way to find fulfillment and purpose."

Heidi thought about what Mark had said for a moment, then nodded in agreement. She thanked him and left the coffee shop, feeling inspired by Mark's consistent positive attitude about life and his willingness to make a difference in the world.

Years went by and Heidi continued to visit the coffee shop regularly. She had taken Mark's advice to heart and had become heavily involved in volunteering and giving back to her community. She had found a new sense of purpose and fulfillment that she had never experienced before. One day, as she walked into the coffee shop, she noticed two new baristas behind the counter. She asked Mark about it, and he explained that he was retiring and had sold the coffee shop to the new baristas. Heidi was sad to hear this, but then realized that Mark had given her something much more valuable than just coffee. He had given her a new perspective on life and had helped her find her purpose. She smiled at the new baristas and said,

"Hey, I'm Heidi! What's your names?"

"Nice to meet you, Heidi! I'm Jacob and this is my younger brother Benjamin."

"You can call me Benny for short." Added Benjamin.

"Great to meet you both." Heidi Replied. "I'm going to miss Mark, but I'm excited to see what you both have in store for this place."

Jacob smiled back and said,

"We have big shoes to fill, but we're up for the challenge!"

As Heidi walked out of the coffee shop, she thought about all of the valuable lessons she had learned from Mark over the years. She realized that she had been given a gift, not just in the form of coffee, but in the form of wisdom and guidance. And she knew that she would continue to pour herself out, just as Mark had taught her to do, in order to make a difference in the world. She was grateful for the lessons she had learned and the memories she had made at the coffee shop. As she walked away, she couldn't help but smile, knowing that Mark's legacy would live on through her and through everyone he had touched with his wisdom and kindness.

Author's Thoughts: The Empty Mug

Throughout my life I've found that one of the most powerful gifts we can give someone, is ourselves. Giving a loved one your full attention when they come to you for advice or giving a stranger direction to a nearby destination that you know like the back of your hand or being present with your children during an episode of play. There's nothing more satisfying than to share a piece of your heart with another.

This is the empty mug.

The longer the coffee sits, the colder it gets. So, it would be wise to focus more on what we can give rather than what we can hold for ourselves.

One of the greatest examples of the self less act of giving is seen in the journey of motherhood. From the moment a woman discovers that she's pregnant, an immediate switch occurs. The mother-to-be will usually make dietary changes, changes to her exercise routine, sleep routine, entertainment choices, travel dreams, career aspirations and other important aspects of her life. And in a way this sacrificial way of living becomes her new way of thinking for the next 20 years or more. A mother pours herself out for the well-being of her children.

Life seems to take note of empty mugs and f inds extraordinary ways of refilling them. This can sometimes happen in the form of rewards, opportunities, gifts, love, kind deeds, good fortune or simply an abundance of joy. I've experienced this empty mug philosophy several times and now it has become an intentional effort that I always try to put forward. In return, I've noticed that whenever I've been in a place where I'm looking for answers or guidance, I've been fortunate enough to learn from successful people I'd have a low probability of ever coming into contact with.

So, how does this usually happen?

I do think it has something to do with the law of reciprocity.

The more you pour out into others, the more is poured into you and this cycle continues.

What will an empty mug look like for you? Will you be more attentive to those who confide in you for advice?

Will you donate your time or resources to those who could benefit from it? Will you be more present with your children when engaging in play? Maybe you'll volunteer at a community center or local fundraiser.

Giving is very for-giving in that it doesn't put any harsh demands on anyone or criticize you when you contribute a little or a lot. It just rewards you when you do it and reminds you of its continual circuit when it circles back to you.

So, don't feel like you can't give because lack of resources. Just give what you can. Give freely, with a cheerful heart even if it's just calling an old friend and grabbing a cup of coffee. You'd be surprised to see how much your life can change when you start emptying your good intentions on others.

I hope this book has been a positive experience for you and more importantly given you a refreshing perspective on how to live an enriched and more robust life.

There's a well-known saying that goes, "wake up and smell the coffee!" If ever you need a simple reminder of what is important and the recipes that make for an enriched life, I hope you pick this book up again and read a few pages and find that awakening scent of things that really matter.

We only get to enjoy one coffee in this life, one brew, one time. Enjoy your coffee and explore every sip and every note. When your coffee is finished and your mug is empty, you'll be very proud of the coffee stains you've left behind and the impressions you've made on the hearts of those you've touched.

Chapter 12

More Coffee Please...

"Go the extra mile, it's never crowded."

– Dr. Wayne Dyer.

This book was written with you in mind. I tasked myself with the responsibility of putting together a modest yet impactful, short book that one could easily open and draw a refined sense of clarity or a refreshing perspective from, no matter where in the book you should land and regardless of your current status in life, relationship or career.

The value proposition to this piece of literature is: A guide to living an enriched life. We can always strive to become a better version of ourselves. I hope you've found at least one take away so far, something simple, actionable, easy to implement or remove from your current way of living. If so, then there's one more happy author somewhere in the world, with an enormous smile on his face.

You're probably thinking, "what a strange way to end a book." And you'd most certainly be right. Luckily however, the book doesn't end here. Just like a fine brew that teases our tastebuds and overwhelms us with satisfaction, it's not uncommon to desire a second cup. It's a fair request and I hope you'll stick around for a little while longer and enjoy some more content with me. I love to write. It's so exciting to position myself in a place where my heart can communicate ideas to my mind. This is why I write and speak and love to communicate. It's one of the most visible transactions of what is brewing inside my heart at any given moment.

And so, in addition to the 11 Simple Truths of how to live an enriched life covered in this book, I thought it would be great to offer some more value by sharing some of my past blogs with you. These blogs cover several topics and themes that really corollate with the contents of this book. I'm confident you'll find extra value in these blogs and actionable takeaways that you can apply to your life. Enjoy.

Chapter 13

Premium Coffee

[Blog: Living a Luxurious Life]

For as long as I can remember, (which I'll quickly admit is not that long ★Hehe) I've always seen or heard the term 'luxury' described according to material wealth, financial exuberance and opulence.

"Look at the size of that house."

"What a luxurious community to live in."

"Wow! look at that yacht or super car."

"Oh, my what a luxurious outfit!" etc. etc.

To be completely honest, I have no problem with it. I think from a qualitative perspective it's kind of cool to see a level of finesse and excellence whether it be in design, price, aesthetic, quality or just the overall experience of what we call luxury.

For example, as a certified tea master sommelier, I'd be the first to distinguish a luxurious Da-Hong Pao Tea, coming in at a whopping 1.2 million dollars per kilo ... Yes, you can breathe now. Or how about an aromatic Tie Guanyin Tea, coming in at $3,000 per kilo as compared to your typical English breakfast or Earl Grey black tea in the grocery store ranging anywhere from $0.99 - $2.00 for a million tea bags. A hyperbole of course. Kind of. But my point is, luxury from this standpoint is exciting and adventurous and worth striving for to create memorable experiences.

But is that the true meaning of luxury?

In 2009, I was the victim of a nearly fatal stabbing by a high-school thug in what started out as a regular fist fight over lyrics to a rap song which quickly escalated to a brutal and extremely violent crime scene. I found myself fighting for my life with four or more stab wounds piercing my body from my neck to my lower abdomen. It was tragic, I had never experienced such pain, trauma and difficulty breathing in my life and yet there I was gasping for every bit of air that I could find. I apologize for the graphic scenario, but it does bring home a very important point about luxury, or at least the true meaning of luxury in my opinion.

On April 16 (a day after the incident) breathing became luxury to me. To wake up and see someone smiling at me after such violent images in my head of fighting and yelling and bloodshed and anger. Healthcare, doctors, nurses and the pleasant staff that made for a clean and enjoyable hospital experience was luxury to me.

Sunshine was luxury to me. Just to look out that St. Michael's Toronto hospital and see birds and buildings and people and planes after enduring the heavy beating of the helicopter's propellers the night before while the paramedics stared at me trying to infuse hope and the will to live into me through gentle, faint smiles.

Family became luxury to me. The warm conversations, visits and support to help me get back to myself, to get back on my feet and to redirect my life in a completely new and inspiring way, while at the same time never making me feel guilty of who I was and where I found myself during that episode of life.

Community is luxury to me. My story has become my message and has been embraced by the community of people around me. Local government officials and dignitaries, friendly neighbours and business owners, students and educational facilitators and even other youth who have found themselves incarcerated or in a tough and similar spot in life have become the people that I now share positive messages of hope with. Through sharing and listening to these unique stories, I have completely changed my views on what it means to live a luxurious life.

So, to answer my own question... A Resounding YES! I do now live a luxurious lifestyle and I encourage you too as well.

With love, Daniel.

Chapter 14

High Mountain Coffee

[Blog: Perspectives on Challenges and obstacles]

"Faith can move mountains, but doubt can create them."

Yet again my dad has directed my attention to a profound quote that is both encouraging and challenging at the same time.

From the moment I entered the world of entrepreneurship and began 'figuring things out' I made it a personal duty of mine to share what I've learned with others. Whether that meant jumping on a quick phone call to offer some advice, delivering a presentation or simply being an open ear to an aspiring entrepreneur looking to bounce their idea off someone else.

One thing I've noticed throughout the years is that there are typically two types of people: 'Mountain Movers' and 'Mountain Makers.' Those who see a challenge as another hurdle to jump over and those who see hurdles as another roadblock of impossibility, too great to overcome.

Mountain Movers

These are people who in most cases (not all) have made a resolve in their life, in their business and in their heart on a specific course of action and are unwilling to be deterred from it. They have weighed the risk of doing and not doing and found the latter to be more lethal. I'm no superhero, but I do my best to cultivate this state of mind.

In business, I believe that every activity that I intend to do will cost me some money, time or effort. This could mean hours, days, weeks and in some cases years. But on the other hand, the cost of inactivity can cost me a lifetime. My inactivity will shape who I am and who I become and personally I feel that these side effects are far worse than just rolling my sleeves up and getting to work on my goals and aspirations.

Do I see mountains?

Absolutely. Every day. Every Idea. But it's what I do when I see them that has equated to my personal success and what I hope to encourage you to do as well. Move them. Try to move them. Get help to move them. Heck! Climb them. Do whatever you have to do to get around it or over it. But don't back down. Practice this mentality and you'll start to find that BIG mountains start to become small hills and eventually bumps in the road.

Mountain Makers

If you're a mountain maker or a person that typically sees a challenge as something too difficult to attempt or overcome, then rest assure this was not written to break you down but instead to help build you up. My hope is that you will take on a new perspective about life, challenges, obstacles and see them as something that can be moved.

Taking risks, stepping out of your comfort zone and trying new things can be extremely difficult and straight up scary, but this doesn't mean it can't be done. It simply means that you're going to have to become bigger than the situation at hand.

How do you become bigger?

There are many was to size up a BIG obstacle in the way.

Consider the bigger picture. I built my business on the foundation of impacting people's lives in a positive way. When the occasional down day happens, sales are low or I'm just not feeling motivated, I consider the lives that I'm able to touch through my business, the communities I'm able to impact and the change I'm able to bring about in the world and suddenly, the balance sheet is put into perspective. Make your goals and aspirations about something bigger.

Don't go at it alone. The saying holds true, there is strength in numbers. You may not be able to take on that BIG BULLY of an obstacle, but what if I help you? What if we help you? What if we all help you? I like to always remind myself that "WE" is stronger than "ME."

Use your size to your advantage

BIG things do what BIG things do. Likewise, small things can do what small things can do. When I started my business, I didn't have the BIG marketing budgets like my competitors did... But I was small enough to move quickly when the industry trends were changing. Whether this meant changing up our product mix or reinventing our brand, I was able to accomplish this in days whereas the BIG players would take months or years to do the same. When all the big animals are watching the sunrise, the ant can get the best seat by climbing the tree.

So, are you a Mountain Mover or a Mountain Maker?

The choice is yours.

Love you all,

Daniel

Chapter 15

Thanksgiving Brew

[Blog: Thankfulness, Gratitude and Appreciation]

Thankfulness is often a realization that hits us when we least expect it. It's a powerful emotion that arises from within us, often in response to a situation or experience that challenges us, forces us to pause, and re-evaluate our perspective.

For example, have you ever had a stuffy nose, and then suddenly been able to breathe clearly again? In that moment, you realize just how amazing it feels to take in a deep breath of fresh air, and you feel grateful for the simple ability to do so. This is the kind of realization that often comes in small moments but can have a big impact on our overall sense of gratitude. Similarly, when your kids are sick or under the weather, you may find yourself feeling grateful for their health and well-being in a way that you didn't before. Suddenly, their naughty behavior seems like a small price to pay for the joy of seeing them happy and healthy again. In other situations, it may be a lack of something that makes us realize how much we truly appreciate it.

When you can't find work, for example, you may start to realize how much you valued your old job, and how lucky you were to have it. This kind of realization can be painful at first, but ultimately it can help us appreciate what we have and motivate us to work harder to achieve our goals. At times, it may be a missed opportunity that makes us realize the value of what we had. If you squander your education, for instance, you may later come to realize the privilege of being taught new things every day is priceless. In such moments, we may feel regret or disappointment, but we can also use that realization to motivate us to work harder and value our opportunities more.

Finally, sometimes it is the struggles of others that help us appreciate what we have. When we see someone struggling to find their next meal, for example, we may realize how much we take for granted the food that is available to us. This kind of realization can be a powerful motivator for us to give back to those in need, to volunteer our time or donate to charity, and to cultivate a sense of gratitude for the blessings in our own lives. In each of these situations, our perspective shifts, and we become aware of the value of what we have in a new way.

It's this back-and-forth perspective of awareness, gratitude or lack thereof that happens everywhere, every day as the world turns. Ultimately, these realizations can help us cultivate a greater sense of thankfulness and lead us to live our lives with more appreciation and purpose.

Chapter 16

Don't Let Your Coffee get Cold!

[Blog: Inspiration Expiration]

"Inspiration has an expiration; it doesn't last forever." - David Heinemeier

When that energetic burst of energy hits your mind, take action. Do something. Begin right away. That "unstoppable-I-can-do-anything" feeling is beautiful when it hits, but when it's gone... it's gone.

"You can accomplish two weeks of work in 24 hours when you're high off inspiration!"

- David Heinemeier Hansson

The amount of quality work you can accomplish in one day when you're inspired, is surprising when you stop and think that it would normally take you a week or two.

So, what are we really doing when we're not inspired?

Why do tasks become so dreary and burdensome?

Where are my superpowers every day when I get my morning started? I have no clue. If I knew the answer to that I'd probably have no need for a fitness app to motivate me to keep my nutrition in check.

But here's my best guess...

Inspiration is a treasure that is half buried in the ground, but always wanting to be found. You can walk right past it, or your curiosity can lead you right to it.

Inspiration is in that book you keep hearing about but haven't read yet.

It's in that person you see feeding birds in the park every day as you pass by on your morning run.

It's in that curious, child you didn't listen to as they try to have a conversation with you.

It's in that beautiful piece of artwork you didn't observe in the hallway you always walk through to get to your next meeting.

It's in that blog you didn't click, that still moment in your backyard you didn't enjoy, because you couldn't find time.

• It's in the harmony of birds chirping as the day breaks while you sleep in.

Inspiration is everywhere. Find it. Use it. Don't ignore it. And remember, when it hits you, ride the wave as long as you can, accomplish as much as you can because when it fades, it fades.

Chapter 17

Short, Grande, Vente?

[Blog: Three Lessons the Tree Taught Me]

If we're willing to listen and we're willing to learn, life can be one of our greatest teachers. Life continues to teach us valuable lessons every day and as I like to say, "you can't skip it's classes."

Yesterday, I took a drive out with my family to enjoy the country road and ref lect. While looking back at a picture I took standing under a tree, I thought...

Instant Gratification

Typically, when we think of the term: "instant gratification" we refer to the desire to experience pleasure or fulfillment without delay. Understanding instant gratification in this way, sometimes makes it difficult or demotivating to start something, build something or plant something, simply because we don't think we'll get to enjoy it right away. However, the tree taught me that many, many years ago, perhaps even before I was born, someone planted that seed and today it stands tall and serves as a moment of ref lection for me. What if the person who planted that tree decided to embrace the satisfaction of knowing that this small seed would one day grow up to offer value, wisdom, shade, or a place of reflection for a stranger they'll most likely never meet. What if that person celebrated the act of kindness and generational investment of planting the tree instead of seeing the tree fully grown? That kind of mindset would offer Instant gratification in so many ways without seeing any physical or tangible evidence.

Self Confidence

If trees were people, a tree in the forest might easily be seen as the "popular kid in school" as it's constantly surrounded by other trees, and all the birds and animals often surround it. But the tree I was standing under, stood alone. So where does that leave this tree? Well, the tree taught me, that it's not always about who's around you and who others say you are that gives you self-confidence. On the contrary, self-confidence comes from the inside and can be seen by the many branches that extend from you. All these branches are the many different things you have explored, the various skills and interests you have, your emotions, your values, the things you're most proud about. These branches are the best reminders that you can become anything you want to be and venture down any path and there is no limit to how many things you can try.

Overtime, your confidence to grow and discover new things, might just inspire some more "trees" to do the same and who knows, they might want to stay closer to you and learn from your experiences, and you'll have your own forest to influence.

Your Perspective on Size

The tree was relatively small to the field in which it stood. If the tree were to consider its size in this way and compare its size and ability to impact according to the field, unfortunately it would come up short. However, the tree taught me, that although it might be small to the field, it was gigantic in the eyes of the ant that would crawl up and down it's hefty trunk every day in search of food. The caterpillar or the bird certainly wouldn't refer to the tree as being "small."

So, perhaps in life you don't have as many "followers" as the Kardashins or you don't have as many credentials as your colleagues, maybe you're not the million-dollar neighbour next door... But who is looking at you? Who is depending on you for ideas, for provision, for inspiration, for comfort, for love and for shelter and shade? Focus on them, take care of them because to them you are a very BIG deal.

"You are as BIG as the impact you leave on the life of another."

Love you all,

Daniel

Chapter 18

These Coffees Never Fail

[Blog: 3 Life Disciplines That Will Never Fail You in Life]

Failure is an inevitable part of life. No matter how much you try to avoid it, you're bound to face it sooner or later. That's why we must learn from every failure and not let them haunt us. Keeping that in mind, here are 3 life disciplines that will never fail you in life. Even when the going gets tough, these practices will help you stay grounded and keep you pushing forward.

The Discipline of Service

There's no better feeling than helping someone in-spite of your own needs. Whether it's a friend or a complete stranger, simply helping others out is a great way to feel fulfilled and see the world through a more positive lens. Even if you don't end up getting anything back in return, just knowing that you made someone's day a little brighter will make you feel great. The discipline of service causes an individual to gain a deeper sense of what true success really means, which many successful role models have collectively stated, true success is all about finding happiness and fulfillment in what you do. If you're ever feeling like you're not successful or that your contributions to life, industry or community are not enough... try contributing to someone else and that feeling will quickly change.

2) The Discipline of Less

Many times, we end up failing simply because we tried to do too much or because we had too high of expectations for ourselves. The overwhelming number of 'things' that we do requires so much focus, attention and energy, that it can be next to impossible to truly execute them successfully. When this feeling occurs, the discipline of less can usually step in and sort things out. Do you really need all of those email accounts? (Talking to myself by the way.) Several business ventures? (Whoops again!) Attending all those meetings? Owning all those properties? As you can imagine, all of these commitments pull on us every single day or at the least take up a lot of room in our mental storage space. The moment one of these responsibilities or commitments begin to fall, we start to feel like we're unsuccessful. Practice cutting the non-essentials out of your life. In the Book Essentialism by Greg McKeown, he tells of the well known stovetop exercise:

If you had 4 stovetops all representing commitments in your life (family, health, career, friends) and you had to turn one off, which would it be?

And if you had to turn off two?

Now of course, this exercise is not designed to make you choose between your family and your health, or your friends and your career, but it should help to give you an idea of your priorities so you can better structure your day, your week, your goals and your life.

The Discipline of Self Development

When you're just starting out in business or your career, you don't have any experience to help you figure things out. That's why you need to learn as much as you can during those early stages. Whether it's from books, the internet, or other people, there's always something new to learn. Moreover, when you're just starting out, you don't have any work experience or reputation to speak of. That means that people are more likely to give you advice and mentorship for free... TAKE IT!

The discipline of self-development in a nutshell is this: You must never stop learning. One of the most valuable and profitable investments I've ever made in my life was my monthly audible subscription. Every month I have access to thousands of books on topics that help to better my life. It's priceless. People pouring out their life experiences, thoughts, perspectives, tactics and wisdom in order to help others do better, get better, live better or see life in a better way. I have disciplined myself to:

A) pay my subscription bill on time

B) soak up as much knowledge and information as I can on various topics that will help me to succeed and live an overall better life. I encourage you to do the same!

Service to others, focus on the essentials a.k.a less and never stop learning. These are 3 relatively simple techniques on paper, but what really matters is what you do with this information. Being disciplined is all about practicing doing what needs to be done, even on the worst days, even when you don't want to. Especially when you don't want to.

Love you guys. Talk soon!

Daniel

Chapter 19

The Perfect Brew

[Blog: 4 Misconceptions We Are Taught About Success]

In today's world, success seems to be a constant pursuit. From early childhood, we're taught that being successful carries with it great sacrifices and great responsibility.

But what if this is all wrong?

The world's most successful people aren't 'extraterrestrial' or from some genius planet that moves at a different frequency. They may have succeeded at something, but that doesn't mean they succeeded because they were smarter, more hardworking, or inherently better than anyone else. Instead, these individuals were successful because they understood how to think like a winner. They knew how to recognize the right opportunities and avoid falling victim to common pitfalls that everyone else has difficulty avoiding.

Now, how can we stop ourselves from sabotaging our own chances of becoming successful? Here's a few culprits that might be holding us back.

The Illusion of Being 'Over-Prepared'

Successful people know that success isn't the product of a single, magical moment. Instead, it's a process of building on each previous success. One of the biggest mistakes that people make is believing that they must be 'over-prepared' for their success. While it's true that you need to be ready for various challenges that may come your way, you don't need to spend infinite amounts of time building a perfect foundation. In today's world, there are endless opportunities that are open to anyone with the right amount of drive and hard work. But if you worry that your success will be jeopardized by a single unassuming mistake, you're not going to make it very far. It's better to keep your focus on the things that you can control, like your daily actions and the state of mind you bring to each one.

You Think You Must Be an Extrovert to Be Successful

Successful people aren't more outgoing than the rest of us. Sure, there is a good number of charismatic leaders and spotlight personalities that are often spoken about in the mainstream media, but that doesn't reflect the entire picture.

Successful people understand that being introverted doesn't prevent them from succeeding. In fact, they have a self-awareness that allows them to be both extroverted and introverted at the same time and understand their strengths and weaknesses. If successful people are extroverted, it's because they know how to use their introverted strengths too. It's all about combining your personality with emotional intelligence and working your talents at the right times and in the right places.

You Mistake Talking for Taking Action

Successful people know that nobody is eager to listen to your ideas until you've already succeeded with them. This is true, but only to a certain extent. From the moment you start dreaming of your future, you subconsciously start building a list of ideas and plans. If you spend all your time trying to explain your ideas to people who don't want to hear them, you're never going to get around to implementing them. Instead, you should be building a network of people who are excited to hear your ideas and willing to help you bring them to reality. And when the time comes for you to present your ideas to the world, nobody will remember how much time you spent explaining them. It's not a million-dollar idea, until it makes a million dollars.

You're Not Building a Community of Supporters

Successful people understand that you don't just have to be hands-on with your ideas. Instead, you must be hands-on with the people and activities that support your ideas. Successful people must be proactive in the areas of their life that matter the most. This includes learning new skills, developing new relationships, and, most importantly, giving back to the community that has supported you. You must be willing to put in the work and create opportunities to connect with other successful people. And most importantly you must be willing to ask them for help when you need it.

Final Sip

The most successful people have a different way of looking at the world, and their success mirrors this. They are creative, outgoing, and open-minded individuals who aren't afraid to step out of their comfort zones. They know that every challenge they face can be overcome with hard work, determination, and a positive attitude. Successful people are willing to take risks, learn new skills, and create new opportunities for themselves. They understand that the path to success isn't always a straight one, and that stumbling is part of the journey.

I hope this can help you to take another look at your current journey to finding success and examine to see if perhaps some of these setback culprits are preventing you from getting ahead. As always, thanks for your time, love you all!

We'll chat soon.

Daniel

Chapter 20

Those Real Beans

[Blog: The Importance of Living an Authentic Lifestyle]

Live authentic. Be authentic. We hear this all the time, but what does it mean?

I guess the best place to start is to define authentic...

Definition: *"of undisputed origin and not a copy;*

genuine." **Aren't We All Authentic Then?**

I mean, we're not all copies of each other, are we?

What makes us who we are? Our family? Our friends? The experiences we have? The things we consume? It could be a combination of all the above really. But let's ask ourselves this. When was the last time, if ever, that you sat down and gave yourself the time and patience to really think about and discover who you are without the influences of your friends, family or society?

Sadly, many would agree that they almost never do that, and of course this is not something intentional... It's just that we sometimes live a life so consumed by today's distractions that we never really give ourselves a chance to know who we really are.

How Can I Get to Know Me?

Above all else, one thing is true. To be authentic, you must be self-aware. Without self-awareness, how can you ever know who you are? What is you? And what is someone else's expectation of you? What is you and what are the limiting beliefs that have been imposed on you from childhood?

Self-awareness is the first and most important step on the journey of self-discovery. I believe one of the best tools for helping you to become more self-aware, is quiet time.

Yes, some call it meditation, but in its simplicity, it is just a time that is less about distractions and more about focus.

These quieter moments have power over the mind and body like nothing else. It allowed me to re-discover myself by asking five personal questions that when answered internally caused me to face the realities of my life and life choices at age twenty-one.

The self-discovery was in fact so deep, I decided to make a complete 360-degree change in my life and how I choose to live it. Quiet time takes you on a journey inside yourself without any external influences, almost like life is holding a big mirror in front of you and all that you can see in the mirror is you. The real you. The authentic you. Quiet time was and still is a very powerful tool to help me center myself and when I feel centered, I feel clarity. When I feel clarity, I feel authentic. When I'm clear, I know myself.

Think of it this way... When you eat a large meal, you feel tired because your body uses most of its energy to break down and process the food you've just eaten. On the other hand, when you haven't eaten for a while, it allows your body to use the energy to heal itself.

Now, think of thoughts, as food. When you have too much information coming in, you get overwhelmed, stressed or anxious. Your mind and body begin to shut down. But what happens when you have minimal information coming in? Your mind can start to zone in or concentrate on other things, on mending and deciphering things that have recently transpired. This offers your mind clarity.

"Ohmmmm!"

Quiet time doesn't have to be sitting down in a dark room, chanting 'Ohm'. It can be anything that allows you to be fully present in the moment, to be free from distraction. For some people, that could be dancing, drawing, writing, exercising or simply partaking in your favourite hobby.

The trick with being authentic is that it's more about stripping away the bad, the old, the limiting beliefs that are no longer wanted or needed than it is about 'adding' qualities.

Remember, we don't have to tell children to be authentic,

do we? No, they just are. We need to strip away all the things this world has given us that stops us from being our authentic selves. We need to be who we were before all those bad things happened to us.

When we think of material items, it's the authentic, genuine, one-of-a-kind products that are the most valuable, while the items that are mass-produced could be bought easily with the change in your pocket.

How can you start your journey on the road to authenticity?

Here's 5 helpful tips to implement today.

- Be genuine. Listen to your heart. Don't let friends, family or circumstances dictate who you can be. Define yourself before others have the chance to define you.

- Find a suitable practice or activity that gives you "quiet time." Anything that frees the mind.

- Never stop learning, never stop evolving.

- Be open to everything, the good and the bad. Don't choose to be ignorant.

- Own everything you do. Authentic people accept their strengths and their weaknesses. They hold themselves accountable.

What is true for me, may not be true for you. You need to find your truth. Never stop seeking your truth. Be open. Be accountable. Be self-aware.

Whatever you do, be kind and compassionate to others. Remember, when you live authentically, you inspire others to do the same.

Love you all,

Daniel

About The Author

Author, entrepreneur and international speaker Daniel Lewis is the proud founder of the award-winning tea company Daniel's Chai bar (formerly known as T By Daniel.) His people-focused outlook on entrepreneurship and his experiential business tactics have garnered him and his company nationwide recognition and many awards and honours such as a 2016 Business Excellence Award and 2017 Top 40 Under 40 Entrepreneurs and 2022 Global Visual Victories Silver Medal for his creative Pop-Up retail Store Design. Daniel's success with his retail tea brand have even landed him an opportunity to serve His Majesty King Charles III during his 2017 Royal Tour in Canada. With his official public speaking platform *iamdaniel.ca* he covers topics on motivational excellence and his non-traditional approaches to retail, marketing, customer service, sales and the world of entrepreneurship with audiences internationally.

Other Books by The Author

How? By Daniel M. Lewis (Autobiography)
Business Lessons from a Teenage Rapper Turned Award WinningEntrepreneur
Available on Amazon.ca and on Audible.

Weird As Waldo
Marketing 101 | How to stand out from the noise
Available on Amazon.ca

QWOTES
Inspiring Quotes | About Business, Entrepreneurship & life.
Available on Amazon.ca

For more info or speaking/booking inquiries
contact **info@iamdaniel.ca www.iamdaniel.ca**

Manufactured by Amazon.ca
Acheson, AB